CW00369587

Boa
Ha

RYA recommended equipment for sail and motor cruising

Revised and updated 2002
by Kathryn Burnett

Photo credits:
Christal clear, Gary Blake and Stephen Lee

Published by
The Royal Yachting Association
RYA House Ensign Way Hamble
Southampton SO41 04YA

Tel: 0845 345 0400
Fax: 0845 345 0329
Email: admin@rya.org.uk
Web: www.rya.org.uk

White
Sept 03
Nottingha.

FOREWORD

Boating is a great sport for people of any age, but there are inherent dangers in going out on the water, whatever the type of boat. Boat safety is largely an attitude of mind, with common sense, education, experience and forward planning playing key parts.

The RNLI urges everyone who goes boating to be properly prepared, which includes having the right safety equipment on board for the type of activity you will be doing.

The RNLI's free Safety Equipment Advisory (SEA) Check Scheme helps you to make the right decision about your boating equipment and our Advisors base their recommendations on the RYA *Boat Safety Handbook*.

I'm sure you will enjoy this book and find it useful. I wish you safe boating.

Andrew Freemantle

Chief Executive

RNLI

CONTENTS

INTRODUCTION

Boating will never be a completely risk free sport. If it was, it would be a rather dull activity and you would probably not be reading this book. Training and experience and the right equipment used properly can help to reduce the risks to an acceptable level.

This book will help you to make an informed choice about what equipment you need on your boat. It is not meant to be a catch all list, but rather a series of recommendations backed up by reasoning and explanation.

There are a number of aspects of boating, other than equipment, that can seriously affect your safety and these are dealt with briefly now.

TRAINING

Your greatest assets are your own skills and experience but these cannot be learnt from a book or by theory alone. Cruising is meant to be challenging but not dangerously so. The RYA offers practical training for all types of boating; motor and sail cruising, powerboating, dinghy sailing and windsurfing. All levels are catered for from complete novice through to Yachtmaster Ocean. There are also shorebased courses available in navigation theory, diesel engine maintenance, VHF, first aid and sea survival. Full details are available from RYA Training - see page 65 for more information.

STRENGTH OF CREW

When planning a cruise, take into account the experience and strength of your crew. For example, novices or young children may not enjoy the physical and mental stresses of a long passage, or sustained rough conditions.

Skippers often forget how challenging it is to be at sea for the first time, let alone if the

conditions deteriorate. Crews suffering from cold, tiredness, hunger and seasickness will not be able to do their job properly. This can result in an over-burdened skipper, and tired skippers make mistakes.

The Marine Accident Investigation Branch (MAIB) has commented a number of times on incidents involving very experienced skippers with almost entirely novice crews. There is nothing wrong with sailing with a novice crew, but always factor in their lack of experience when passage planning and ensure that they have a full safety brief before departure.

YACHT DESIGN AND STABILITY

Take into account the basic design of your boat when deciding whether it is capable of a specific cruise. Boats sold in Europe since June 1998 will be categorized under the EU Recreational Craft Directive (RCD) (see page 8). These categories give an indication of the sorts of conditions your boat was designed to withstand. If your boat was built prior to the RCD coming into effect, or is exempt from the directive, you will have to make your own assessment about what it is capable of.

Be aware of the affect that some equipment, such as radar antennas and reflectors, teak decks, roller jibs etc, can have on the stability of your boat. Any weight added above the boat's centre of gravity will act as a heeling moment and will affect the stability of your boat. This 'top hamper' effect will be particularly marked on motor yachts because, unlike sail cruisers, they do not have ballast to provide a counter balance. If in doubt, take advice from an expert before you fit the equipment.

There is more information about stability and buoyancy in the RYA publication *Stability and Buoyancy*, (G23). To order see page 58/59.

REGULATIONS FOR NON-COMMERCIAL PLEASURE CRAFT

Non-commercial leisure boating in the UK is largely unregulated, although there are some regulations that you do need to know about and comply with.

Regulations applying to private, pleasure boats (ie non-commercial) owned by UK nationals are:

All boats: **SOLAS V**
Harbour authority byelaws and regulations
EU Recreational Craft Directive (RCD)
Pollution - MARPOL

Plus: **Boats over 13.7m (45 feet) - UK Merchant Shipping Regs**
Boats used on UK inland waters
Racing yachts

These regulations are dealt with in more detail below.

SOLAS Chapter V - from 1 July 2002

The exact wording of the regulations is used with some explanatory notes provided by the RYA.

Radar reflector - *Regulation 19.2.1.7.*

A basic radar reflector

All ships shall have, if less than 150 gross registered tonnes and if practicable, a radar reflector or other means, to enable detection by ships navigating by radar at both 9 and 3 GHz.

RYA Note: 'When practicable' means that if you can carry a radar reflector, you should. Both passive radar reflectors and active devices are available - there are advantages and disadvantages to both types and there is more discussion on page 22.

Lifesaving signals - *Regulation 29.*

An illustrated table describing the life-saving signals shall be readily available to the officer of the watch on every ship to which this chapter applies. The signals shall be used by ships or persons in distress when communicating with life-saving stations, maritime rescue units and aircraft engaged in SAR ops.

RYA Note: Keeping this table on board will mean that you comply with this regulation - the table can be found on pages 50/51. It is also available from a number of other sources - contact RYA Cruising for more information.

Danger messages - *Regulation 31.*

Masters are to communicate information on navigational dangers. These include, for example, a dangerous derelict or other dangerous obstructions, tropical storms, winds of Force 10 or more for which no warning has been received. The form that information is sent is not obligatory and it can be transmitted in plain language or using the International Code of Signals. Contracting governments must promulgate any danger information received and messages must be free of charge to ships.

RYA Note: This regulation basically means that you, as skipper, have a responsibility to pass on information about navigation dangers to the Coastguard by any means that you can.

Danger messages - *Regulation 32.*

This regulation deals with the kind of information required in danger messages. It also has examples of typical danger messages.

RYA Note: This regulation means that you should pass on sufficient information about any navigation dangers you experience or witness (For example: position, nature of danger, time seen/witnessed, any other useful information) to enable other shipping in the area to avoid it.

Distress messages - *obligations and procedures - Regulation 33.*

Masters are obliged to respond to distress messages from any source. Ships can be requisitioned by the master of a ship in distress or the Search and Rescue (SAR) authorities.

RYA Note: This regulation reinforces the duty of skippers to respond to any distress messages they hear.

Safe navigation and avoidance of dangerous situations - *Regulation 34.*

Voyage planning is required on all vessels that go to sea. 'Going to sea' is defined as proceeding outside of categorized waters. You can get more information about what constitutes categorised waters from the MCA and the RYA.

MCA guidance notes say for 'small craft and pleasure vessels, the degree of voyage planning will be dependent on the size of vessel, its crew and the length of the voyage'. The MCA says that it 'expects all mariners to make a careful assessment of any proposed voyage taking into account all dangers to navigation, weather forecasts, tidal predictions and other relevant factors including the competence of the crew.'

RYA Note: Skippers should note that this regulation changes the status of passage planning on small boats from simply good practice to a requirement under UK law. No formal written plan is required and there is no set format. Anyone who goes on an RYA practical course will be confident of their ability to plan a cruise competently. Anyone who is not confident of their passage planning ability should take a suitable RYA practical course. (see page 65 for more details).

Misuse of distress signals - *Regulation 35.*

Distress signals only to be used for the proper purpose.

RYA Note: This regulation reinforces the fact that distress signals have a life saving role and should not be misused.

Harbour authority byelaws and regulations

Harbour Authorities may have local byelaws in force for leisure boats such as speed limits within the harbour. It is best to check what these are as part of your passage planning.

Some Harbour Authorities may have their own website and publish small boat guides. In addition, there are usually details of byelaws in almanacs and pilot books. The more important rules, such as speed limits are posted up on notices within the harbour.

Useful websites:

Port of London Authority: www.portoflondon.co.uk
Port of Southampton: www.abports.co.uk
Harwich Haven Authority: www.hha.co.uk

 ## EU recreational craft directive (RCD)

Since 16 June 1998, all recreational craft, with few exceptions, between 2.5 and 24 metres in length, imported into the EEA for the first time, and home-built boats if placed on the market within five years of completion, have to comply with the essential requirements of the RCD and must be CE marked to certify this compliance. The builder, his agent or the person importing the boat is responsible for such compliance and marking. For more information about the RCD, including how to get your imported boat CE marked, contact RYA Technical, see page 47 for details.

Pollution - MARPOL

This international regulation says that no waste should be put over the side under any circumstances. Under a new EU directive, all vessels will have to put waste in a waste reception facility before leaving port. There is more information on the MCA's website - MSN 1720 has the details or call the RYA Cruising Department for a copy of the *Tide Lines* leaflet.

Vessels over 12m are obliged to have information about MARPOL regulations on board. RYA Cruising has more information, see page 47 for contact details.

Boats over 13.7m (45 feet) LOA - UK Merchant Shipping Regulations

Private vessels of more than 13.7m LOA must carry certain items of equipment by law. Details are available from the RYA (and its website) and the MCA, see page 47 for details.

Note that the equipment required may be in excess of that described on pages 10-13 of this book.

Boat Safety

Boats used on UK inland waters

If you plan to use your boat on the UK's inland waters, you will be subject to the Boat Safety Standards and your boat must be certificated to the UK Boat Safety Scheme. British Waterways, the Environment Agency and the Broads Authority issue these regulations jointly. Sea-going boats are exempt for two visits of 28 days per year. See page 47 for useful contacts.

Offshore yacht racing

Offshore racing yachts must comply with the relevant regulations. RYA publication *Racing Yacht Safety, YR9* has details and is available from the RYA, see page 47 for details.

Maritime and Coastguard Agency

Boats in commercial use (charter, sea schools etc)

Boats used commercially (sea schools, charter boats) that go to sea DO have to comply with the MCA Codes of Practice.

More details on the Codes of Practice are available from the RYA or from the MCA. Copies of the codes are available from RYA Despatch and from HMSO - see page 47 for more details.

VESSEL CATEGORIES

A cruiser setting off to go round the world will obviously face greater hazards than a dinghy used for day cruising or a motorboat used for inshore fishing trips.

The speed of the vessel must also be taken into account when selecting its category. For instance, a motor cruiser owner might think that he is within Category C because of the sort of cruising he does, whereas the speed of his boat puts him in Category B because of the greater distances he can cover in a given time.

Each type of equipment is explained and considered in more detail on pages 16-44.

Category A - ocean
Boats that make ocean passages of any length.

Boats in this category are likely to be larger than 10m LOA. Boats over 13.7m (45 feet) LOA are subject to Merchant Shipping regulations for some equipment - see page 9 for details.

Category B - offshore
Boats that cruise around the British Isles and NW Europe, making offshore passages of between 50 and 500 miles.

Boats in this category are likely to be between 8m and 13.7m LOA.

Category C - inshore
Boats that cruise along the coast, within 10 miles of land and within approximately four hours passage time of a safe harbour of refuge in which shelter may be found, by day or night.

Boats in this category are likely to be under 8m LOA.

Category D - sheltered waters
Boats that operate in daylight only, in estuaries, inshore or inland waters, close to a safe harbour of refuge in which shelter may be found within about one hour in worsening weather.

On certain coastlines, notably in the Bristol Channel and on the north east coast, where most of the harbours dry out at low water and no secure anchorages are available in onshore winds, Category D scales of equipment may be inappropriate unless you are sailing only in settled, fine weather, in limited areas.

Boats in this category are likely to be under 6m LOA, but inland motor cruisers may be of any length.

The table on pages 11 to 13 is applicable to vessels up to 13.7m (45 feet) LOA. For vessels bigger than this, see page 9 for further information.

Recommended Safety Equipment for boats up to 13.7m LOA

		CATEGORY			
		A	B	C	D
1.	**Means of propulsion**				
1.1	For craft under 6m in length, oars or paddles, for use in calms, (sailing craft) or in the event of engine failure (power driven craft)			•	•
1.2	For sailing yachts only, a storm trisail or deep reef in the mainsail. See page 17 for details	•	•	•	
1.3	For sailing yachts fitted with auxiliary engines. Either a battery whose sole purpose is to start the engine, which is isolated from all other electrical systems, or a means of starting the auxiliary by hand	•	•	•	
2.	**Anchors**				
2.1	Anchor(s) with length of warp and chain or chain only appropriate to the cruising area and a diameter appropriate to the size of the yacht	2+	2	2	1
2.2	Anchoring fittings to include:				
	(a) A fairlead at the stem capable of being closed over the anchor warp or chain	•	•	•	
	(b) A strong point, on the foredeck, either a mooring cleat, sampson post or anchor winch, securely fitted to the structure of the hull	•	•	•	•
3.	**Bailing and bilge pumping**				
3.1	A hand bailer				1
3.2	Bucket(s) of not less than 9 litres (1.2 gallon) and not more than 14 litres (3 gallon) capacity fitted with a lanyard and a strongly secured handle	2	2	2	
3.3	Hand bilge pumps discharging overboard, and capable of operation with all hatches closed	2	2	1	
	(an electric or engine driven bilge pump may be fitted in place of one hand-operated pump for category B or A yachts)				
3.4	Softwood plugs attached adjacent to all through hull fittings	•	•	•	•
3.5	All through hull fittings able to be closed	•	•	•	
4.	**Detection equipment**				
4.1	A radar reflecting device, properly mounted with as large a radar cross section as can reasonably be carried (see page 6 also)	•	•	•	•
4.2	Fixed navigation lights which comply with the International Regulations for Preventing collisions at Sea	•	•	•	
	including: - motoring cone (sail only)	•	•	•	•
	anchor ball and light	•	•	•	•
4.3	A sound signalling appliance (foghorn)	•	•	•	
4.4	Powerful torch ('steamer scarer')	•	•	•	
5.	**Pyrotechnics (in date)**				
5.1	Hand-held red flares	6	4	4	2
5.2	Buoyant orange smoke signals	2	2		
5.3	Red parachute rockets	12	4	2	
5.4	Hand-held orange smoke signals			2	2
5.5	Hand-held white flares -not available worldwide	4	4	4	

Items 5.1 – 5.3: } To SOLAS standards

6   Fire fighting equipment

	Col1	Col2	Col3	Col4
6.1 Fire blanket, for all yachts with cooking equipment. (BS EN 1869)	•	•	•	•
6.2 For yachts either fitted with a galley or carrying fuel for an engine multi-purpose extinguishers of minimum fire rating 5A/34B (to BS EN 3)	3	2	1	1
6.3 Additionally, for yachts fitted with both a galley and carrying fuel for an engine, multi-purpose extinguishers of minimum fire rating 5A/34B (to BS EN 3)	1	1	1	1
6.4 Additionally, for yachts with high powered (over 25.h.p.) engines a fixed automatic or semi-automatic fire fighting system installed to discharge in to the engine space	•	•	•	•
6.5 Additionally, for all boats at least one multi-purpose fire extinguisher of minimum fire rating 113A/113B or smaller extinguishers giving the equivalent fire rating (to BS EN 3) - see page 25 for more details	•	•	•	

7.   Personal safety equipment for each member of the crew:

	Col1	Col2	Col3	Col4
7.1 Warm clothing, oilskins, seaboots and hat	•	•	•	•
7.2 A lifejacket or a buoyancy aid (BS EN 395) 100 Newtons				1
7.3 A lifejacket (BS EN 396) 150 Newtons	1	1	1	
7.4 Lifejacket light	1	1		
7.5 Spray face cover	1	1		
7.6 A safety harness (for yachts with an enclosed wheelhouse, one harness each for 50% of the crew (BS EN 1095)	1	1	1	
7.7 Immersion suit - per crew member	1			
7.8 Jackstays and cockpit clip on points	•	•	•	

8.   Liferaft

	Col1	Col2	Col3	Col4
8.1 A liferaft designed for the sole purpose of saving life, of sufficient capacity to carry everyone on board	1	1	1	
8.2 An emergency grab-bag (see page 32 for contents)	1	1	1	

9.   Man overboard recovery equipment

	Col1	Col2	Col3	Col4
9.1 Horseshoe lifebelts fitted with drogue and self-igniting light	2	2	1	
9.2 Buoyant sling on floating line - may replace one horseshoe life-belt if two are carried	1	1		
9.3 A buoyant heaving line, at least 30m in length, with quoit	1	1	1	
9.4 A boarding ladder capable of rapid and secure attachment	1	1	1	
9.5 A dan buoy with a large flag	1	1		

10.   Radio

	Col1	Col2	Col3	Col4
10.1 A radio receiver, capable of receiving shipping forecasts on 198kHz and weather forecasts broadcast by local radio stations	1	1	1	1
10.2 A marine-based VHF radio telephone	1	1	1	1
10.3 Digital Selective Calling (DSC) controller to R&TTE directive standards	1	1	1	
10.4 A marine-band HF/SSB radio and/or global satellite communications system	1			
10.5 406 MHz EPIRB - registered in the name of the vessel	1			

10.6 Navtex	1	1	1	
10.7 Radio transponder (SART)	1			
10.8 Emergency VHF radio aerial with a prepared deck mounting	1	1		
10.9 Waterproof VHF hand-held radio	1	1	1	1
11. Navigational equipment				
11.1 Up-to-date charts of the local area and a local tide table				•
11.2 Up-to-date charts, tide tables and navigational publications of the intended cruising area and adjacent areas into which the yacht may go under stress of weather	•	•	•	
11.3 Steering compass - able to be lit at night	1	1	1	1
11.4 Hand-bearing compass	•	•	•	
11.5 Navigational drawing instruments including parallel rulers, or a plotting instrument and dividers	1	1	1	
11.6 Barometer	1	1	1	
11.7 Lead line and echo sounder	1	1	1	
11.8 Radio navigation system e.g. GPS	1	1	1	1
11.9 A watch or clock	1	1	1	1
11.10 Distance measuring log	1	1	1	
11.11 Binoculars	1	1	1	
11.12 Sextant and tables	1			
12. First aid kit				
A first aid kit and manual (see text for contents)	1	1	1	1
13. General equipment				
13.1 Emergency tiller on all wheel steered vessels	1	1	1	1
13.2 Towing warp (not required if anchor warp is carried)	1	1	1	
13.3 Mooring warps and fenders	•	•	•	•
13.4 A waterproof torch	3	2	2	1
13.5 A rigid or inflatable tender	•	•	•	
13.6 Tool kits for general, engine, electrical and sail repairs	•	•	•	•
13.7 Spares for engine and electrics, and bosun's bag of shackles and twine	•	•	•	•
13.8 Emergency water supply, isolated from main tanks	•	•		
13.9 Emergency repair materials	•	•		
13.10 Bosun's chair (sit harness BS EN 813 1997)	1	1	1	

NOTE:

a) Where a number appears it refers to the recommended numbers of that item to be carried.

b) Where • appears it simply recommends that the item be carried but the number, method or contents is left to the judgement of the skipper.

PREPARATION AND PLANNING

It is a false and potentially dangerous economy to skimp on preparation, however experienced you are and whatever the length of your trip.

Training

Training and experience are key to safety at sea and we highly recommend that you take an appropriate RYA training course (see pages 56/57 for more details).

Maritime and Coastguard Agency

Coastguard voluntary safety information scheme (CG66)

This is a free scheme that helps the Coastguard to help you, should you get into trouble. By registering with the scheme, vital time can be saved in a potential search and rescue situation. A form, together with information on how you can join the scheme, is attached inside this book (see pages 52-55). The RYA recommends that anyone who goes cruising joins this scheme. Alternatively, let someone at home know your plans, together with a rough ETA.

Safety Equipment Advisory Check

RNLI SEA Check

This is another free safety scheme. The RNLI will send a specially trained expert to check your boat and the safety equipment you have on board and offer you advice about improvements or changes. The equipment levels they recommend are based on those in this book. Call 0800 328 0600 for details.

Voyage planning

This is now a requirement on all pleasure boats that go to sea (see SOLAS V, page 6). The following factors, among others, should be considered:

• Weather forecasts

• Tidal information

• Planned route using charts and pilotage information

• Strength of crew

• Capabilities of boat

For more information on passage planning, you can find out more in a number of RYA publications or go on a RYA training course (see page 65 for more details).

Check your engine

If you rely on your engine, regularly check your fuel and oil level and the state of your fuel filter. If you have a diesel engine onboard, consider taking the RYA Diesel Engine Course (see pages 56/57 for more details).

Brief your crew

A non-existent or poor crew brief by skippers has been considered to be a contributory factor in many leisure boating incidents investigated by the Marine Accident Investigation Branch (MAIB).

Show all crew, however experienced, where safety equipment is stowed and how to use it.

Allocate everyone on board a lifejacket and harness, which should be adjusted to fit before you depart.

Ensure the crew know how to use galley equipment safely and are properly briefed on man overboard procedures and other safety drills.

The importance of properly briefing all crew cannot be overstressed.

EQUIPMENT

STOWAGE AND MAINTENANCE

You are likely to need safety equipment in the worst possible conditions, maybe when it's dark and probably when you are experiencing severe weather. So, it is important to properly maintain all safety equipment on board and to stow it within easy reach.

Have a methodical approach to maintenance. Some safety items such as liferafts will need professional servicing by authorised companies. You will be able to maintain other pieces of equipment yourself. Service your engine regularly and do some basic checks each time you go cruising.

MEANS OF PROPULSION

Mechanical failure is still the main cause of distress in both motor and sailing boats. Ideally, all boats should have two independent, all weather means of propulsion. Most sailing cruisers will have a choice of sails and an auxiliary engine.

Ideally, every sea-going motor yacht will have two totally independent engines, each with its own isolated electrical system and fuel and water supplies.

For smaller sail or motor boats, an independent outboard is a reasonable alternative. If your motor boat has only one engine, you should be aware of the reliance you have on it for your safety. Maintenance is particularly important and if there is any doubt about its condition or reliability, resolve the problem before setting out.

Very small boats can be propelled using paddles or oars if the conditions are favourable. Oars need rowlocks fitted to be effective, whereas paddles are only effective on very small boats up to approximately 5m LOA.

On shallow inland waters a pole or punt can be used for boats of most lengths. It is unrealistic to rely on paddles or oars to propel you for more than short distances - just enough to get you out of immediate danger.

Propellers

A fouled propeller will effectively cause engine failure. There are gadgets available that can be fitted to propellers to cut away obstructions and prevent fouling; these are often advertised in the yachting press.

It's a good idea to carry a dive mask and snorkel (and even a wetsuit) so that someone can go overboard and try to clear an obstruction. Obviously, the safety of an individual should never be compromised.

Sail cruisers - storm sails

Storm sails are essential for coastal and offshore cruisers. They enable a yacht to be sailed off a lee shore in a strong wind. Storm sails must be small enough to reduce the heeling moment in a strong wind to an acceptable limit and they must be efficient so that they produce a sufficient amount of drive, despite their small size. A sail maker will be able to give you advice on the correct size and weight of storm sails for your boat.

Even boats with roller-reefed sails should have storm sails that can work independently of the furling gear. Although the furling gear is usually very simple, it is still a mechanical device and more prone to failure under adverse conditions than a basic system of lashings. Also, roller reefed sails tend to become fuller and baggier as the sail is rolled, which is the wrong shape for windward efficiency.

A heavy weather mainsail can either take the form of a deep reef in the sail (reducing the sail area by at least 40%) or a trisail. The advantage of a trisail is that it can be made of heavier cloth than you might want in your mainsail and it can be used if the main is torn or the boom broken. Disadvantages are: additional cost, extra stowage space and the physical strength needed to set it, which may be challenging on a short handed cruising boat in bad weather.

A set of deep-reef points in the main, together with the necessary boom fittings and reefing lines, is a cheaper and simpler alternative, although it depends on the mainsail and the boom remaining intact.

A storm jib usually requires special sheet leads because it needs to be sheeted well inboard and forward of the positions used for light weather and working sails. It will also generally require a (probably removable) separate forestay if a roller jib is fitted. Storm jibs need considerable halyard tension to keep the luff straight and this needs to be taken into consideration when designing the halyard rig for it.

Bright red or fluorescent orange storm sails will increase the visibility of your yacht in rough seas and bad weather.

As discussed above, the rigging for storm sails differs from that of ordinary working sails. As with any safety drill, practice how to rig them in fine weather rather than waiting until you really need them.

Three reefs give a main that will reef up to 60% of its total area.

Trisail

A very small strong sail rigged instead of the main in very strong winds.

ANCHORS, CABLES AND ANCHOR DECK FITTINGS

Types of anchor

The importance of anchors cannot be over emphasised; when all else has failed it is only your anchor that will hold your boat off the rocks.

There are two families of anchor; the digging type (eg: Bruce, CQR, Meon, Delta, Danforth) and the surface holding type (Fishermans and Grapnel).

Bruce

Good holding-to-weight ratio. Awkward to stow in a small anchor locker.

Delta

Good holding-to-weight ratio. Designed to stay on bow roller for self launching.

Danforth

Good holding-to-weight ratio. Stows flat, can be hard to break out of mud.

Fishermans

Traditional type, good for rocky & weedy bottoms. Awkward to stow and poor holding power in sand and mud.

CQR or Plough

Good holding-to-weight ratio. Hard to stow and moving parts can capsize.

Digging anchors are very efficient and produce good holding power for a relatively light weight. They are very popular as they give good, all round performance. They tend to hold well in mud, clay, sand and, to some extent, stones.

Some designs may have the disadvantage that, if they break out and drag, they may take seabed material with them and continue to drag rather than digging in again. The Bruce, which was designed to hold North Sea Oil Rigs, is probably the exception, as it seems to dig back in again quite quickly.

The different designs of digging anchors all have their own advantages and disadvantages, so understand the limitations of the equipment you choose to have on board and use it accordingly. The difference in holding power in mud between the digging and surface types of anchor is about 7:1 in favour of the digging type.

Surface holding anchors are relatively inefficient and so a much heavier anchor is needed to produce the same holding power as an equivalent digging anchor. Their advantage is that if they drag they do tend to dig in again and they are also more suited to certain types of holding ground such as rock and coral, and due to their greater weight, can usually be relied on to penetrate sea grasses and weeds.

The table below gives the recommended mass of anchor for the size of your boat. You may choose to carry a heavier anchor than is recommended; for example, more weight is needed to penetrate heavy weed and for riding out storms (particularly if you cruise in the Tropics).

Bower and kedge anchors

Cruising boats are usually equipped with a heavy bower anchor and a lighter kedge. The bower anchor is the main anchor and used for overnight anchorages or whenever the boat is left unattended.

The kedge is used when the full holding power of the anchor is not needed; for example, when anchoring just for an hour or so.

It is also useful to have a lighter anchor that can be deployed using the dinghy if the yacht grounds, when it would be impossible to use the bower and its heavy chain cable. In such a situation a kedge anchor with warp cable, is the ideal compromise between lightness for ease of handling and weight for holding power.

The table below is the DoT requirements for the minimum size of a conventional digging type of anchor and its cable. A motor cruiser or catamaran, both of which have higher windage, should increase anchor specification by at least 25%.

LOA + LWL / 2	Anchor Mass		Anchor Cable Diameter			
	Main	Kedge	Main		Kedge	
			Chain	Rope	Chain	Rope
(metres)	(kg)	(kg)	(mm)	(mm)	(mm)	(mm)
6	8	4	6	12	6	10
7	9	4	8	12	6	10
8	10	5	8	12	6	10
9	11	5	8	12	6	10
10	13	6	8	12	6	10
11	15	7	8	12	6	10
12	18	9	8	14	8	12
13	21	10	10	14	8	12
14	24	12	10	14	8	12
15	27	13	10	-	8	12
16	30	15	10	-	8	12
17	34	17	10	-	8	14
18	38	19	10	-	8	14
19	42	21	12	-	10	14
20	47	23	12	-	10	14
21	52	26	12	-	10	14
22	57	28	12	-	10	16
23	62	31	12	-	10	16
24	68	34	12	-	10	16

Notes:
1. Chain cable diameter given is for short link chain. Chain cable should be sized in accordance with EN 24 565:1989 (covering ISO 4565:1965 and covered by BS 7160:1990 - Anchor chains for small craft), or equivalent.
2. The rope diameter given is for nylon construction. When rope of another construction is proposed, the breaking load should be not less than that of the nylon rope specified in the table.
3. When anchors and cables are manufactured to imperial sizes, the metric equivalent of the anchor mass and the cable diameter should not be less than the table value.

Anchor cable - chain or warp?

The choice between chain or warp depends on how keen you are to keep your boat light for high performance. Chain is more efficient, but warp is lighter.

If you use warp, have at least 5m of chain between the anchor and the warp. This will minimise chafe and help to keep the stock of the anchor horizontal. If the angle of the stock is raised above the horizontal, the anchor's holding power will be reduced. If the angle increases too much, the anchor will eventually break out and drag.

Chain will keep your boat more stationary than warp when anchored in a tideway or breeze. Warp may become fouled around the keel, rudder or propeller when anchored in a wind against tide situation.

A good compromise is to use 12m of heavy chain, about twice the recommended diameter,

between the anchor and the warp. The scope of cable to use with this arrangement is similar to that which would be used with chain.

Use warp for the kedge, as it is essential to be able to lay it using the dinghy. Nylon is best for anchor warp as it stretches and so can absorb the shock loads.

The amount of cable to carry on board your boat depends on your cruising area and the depth of water you are likely to anchor in: 100m of chain or 150m of warp should be sufficient to anchor in a depth of 25m at high water.

Many yachtsmen use a simple rule of thumb for deciding the scope, or length, of cable to deploy when anchoring:

4 x depth of water at HW, when anchoring with chain.
6 x depth of water at HW, when anchoring with warp.

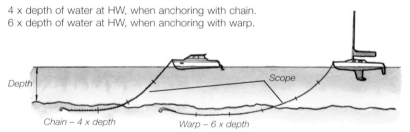

Depth

Scope

Chain – 4 x depth

Warp – 6 x depth

These rules are only very rough and ready guides. They tend to lead to too little cable deployment at depths up to about 15m and the impression that it is impractical to anchor in greater depths due to lack of cable. In reality, the amount of cable you deploy will depend on many factors, such as the depth of water, type of anchor and cable you use, weather conditions, type of holding and how long you plan to stay. Anchoring is an art rather than a precise science so experience and practice (and training, if necessary) will improve your skill.

Deck fittings

These are just as important as the anchor and cable themselves. There should be a bow fairlead, which can be closed over the top of the cable (often with a heavy pin) to prevent it jumping out of the fairlead as the boat pitches. Some older boats will have a sampson post on the foredeck.

The loads imposed by anchor and cable can be very severe, so the deck fitting you secure them to must be firmly attached to the main structure of the boat. For example, don't rely on a cleat bolted to a GRP deck, unless you know that it has a large reinforcing or backing pad. For similar reasons, relying on a winch brake or pawl is not safe - you must take a number of turns of chain to secure the anchor cable.

BILGE PUMPS

The ideal bilge pumping system has two pumps; one on deck and one below. Both should operate with all hatches and washboards in place and each should have its own suction and discharge lines.

If a pump is in the cockpit or on deck, stow its handle close by and secure it with a retaining lanyard so that it can't be accidentally dropped overboard. Carry a spare diaphragm and non-return valve for each pump in your spares kit.

Many boats are fitted with electric bilge pumps that switch on automatically when the water in the bilge reaches a certain level. These are very good for coping with small amounts of water, such as a weep through the stern gland, but cannot be relied on in emergencies when electrical power may not be available.

Always carry a hand operated pump to cover the worst eventuality. The simplest form of manual pump is a crew member and a bucket - and this should not be overlooked in an emergency - but is not an ideal alternative to a hand pump because it requires an open hatch or companionway.

BE SEEN - DETECTION EQUIPMENT

Navigation Lights

The navigation lights on your boat must comply with the detailed specifications in the International Regulations for Preventing Collisions at Sea (IRPCS or COLREGS). It is illegal for vessels to use navigation lights that do not comply with these regulations.

You can find more details about IRPCS in the RYA book *The International Regulations for Preventing Collisions at Sea, (G2/02).* See page 58/59 for more information.

Carry spare bulbs and other electrical spares when cruising in case your lights fail.

In close quarters with other boats or in restricted waters and harbours, high masthead tri-lights can easily be mistaken for lights on shore. Deck mounted navigation lights and stern lights are more easily seen in such circumstances. If possible, fit both types and switch to the most appropriate set for the environment that you are in.

Passive and Active Radar Reflectors

Merchant Ships tend to rely very heavily on radar for detecting other vessels, so you should maximise your boat's radar echo. Boats themselves do not provide a very good radar echo so a radar reflector (passive device) or a radar target enhancer (active device) is needed to boost your boat's radar echo. Since 1 July 2002, all ships less than 150 gross tons are required by law to fit such devices 'if practicable' - see SOLAS V page 6.

Passive reflectors tend to be a variation on the octahedral form, although many modern models are 'stacked arrays'. These are clusters of octahedrals encased in an outer cover of GRP, and tend to look a bit like a fender. There are lens models available, but these tend to be more expensive than the octahedral ones.

There has been much debate in the yachting press about the effectiveness of passive reflectors, which is hotly contested by the manufacturers. The basic rule is that reflectors should be as big as you are able to fit and ideally have more than a 10m^2 radar cross section (RCS). Fit your octahedral reflector in the 'rain catching' position (see diagram on page 6) and at least 4m above the waterline, or as high as you can fit it.

Active devices are known as radar target enhancers or RTEs. These are permanently mounted, powered devices that detect radar illumination and return a strong, consistent echo. Generally, they give a more consistent radar echo than passive reflectors. Their disadvantages are that they rely on power, albeit a small source, and so would not work if the boat's power fails and they do not work in the S-band of radar, which is what large commercial ships rely on in bad weather conditions to see through the 'radar clutter'. RTEs complement passive reflectors, they do not replace them, so ideally carry both.

PYROTECHNICS (DISTRESS FLARES)

Distress flares have two functions:

• To raise the alarm.

• To pinpoint the position of a vessel in distress.

The firing mechanisms of flares differ according to the manufacturer's instructions. Learn how to fire your flares and brief your crew about where they are stored and how and when to use them.

The RYA recommends that flares complying to SOLAS standards are used where applicable. This information is usually indicated somewhere on the side of each flare.

Flare storage

Flares should be immediately available, as you may have no warning before a distress situation occurs. Store them in a suitable container and in a dry place as they will degrade in a damp, salty atmosphere.

A number of flares can be clipped onto the bulkhead alongside the companionway, with the remainder in a watertight box ready to take on deck or into the liferaft, if necessary.

Flares are marked with their date of manufacture and expiry date. Out of date pyrotechnics become progressively less reliable and lose their colour, brilliancy and burn-time. Always have enough in-date flares and keep some newly out of date flares as reserves.

Out of date pyrotechnics must be returned to the manufacturer or the Coastguard for proper disposal, free of charge. RYA Cruising has details of your nearest disposal site.

Distress flares

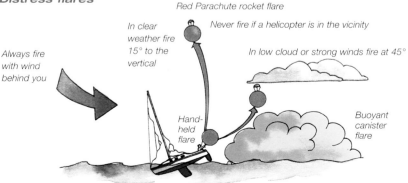

Red Parachute rocket flare

In clear weather fire 15° to the vertical

Never fire if a helicopter is in the vicinity

Always fire with wind behind you

In low cloud or strong winds fire at 45°

Hand-held flare

Buoyant canister flare

Parachute rocket flare

The parachute rocket is the most effective flare for raising the alarm - particularly at night. It projects a very bright flare to a height of about 300m, which burns for 40 seconds while the flare drifts down on a parachute. The rocket will seek into wind during its upward trajectory. It should be fired downwind at an angle of about 15° to the vertical. Never fire a parachute rocket flare if a helicopter is in the vicinity.

Hand-held red flare

This is a pinpoint flare; its main function is to indicate precisely the position of a vessel in distress when help is on the way. It is less bright than a parachute flare and will burn for about one minute.

The flare gives off burning dross and so should be held downwind, outboard and tilted away from the operator. Be aware that the dross could ignite fuel if there is a leak.

Orange smoke signal

This is also a pinpoint flare and an alternative to a hand-held red flare, for use in bright sunlight. Orange smoke is particularly useful for indicating distress to aircraft. Two types are available; a hand-held model (these are only available on the leisure market and are not SOLAS approved). They tend to have a similar firing mechanism to hand-held red flares. The second type is a buoyant, canister which is activated and then thrown overboard to leeward.

Mini-flares

These are short-burn, projected flares. They come in cartridges and are fired with a screw-on penjector, which has a trigger mechanism. Their packaging makes them handy to have on board (and to keep in an oilskin pocket in case you are separated from the boat), but their short burn time of 5-8 seconds is a disadvantage.

Hand-held white flare

This is not a distress flare and is not SOLAS approved. They are used to draw attention to a yacht's presence, particularly if it is on a collision course with a large ship that does not seem to be taking avoiding action. A couple of the flares are best kept clipped on the bulkhead inside the companionway so that they can be grabbed in an emergency, close-quarters situation.

Verey pistols

These are not very common nowadays. They are excluded from the UK ban on firearms, but do require a firearms certificate and a strong box for storage. Cartridges do not have the same duration or visibility as flares so double the number should be carried.

FIRE FIGHTING

Fire Hazards

The two main fire hazards in a yacht are petrol vapour and liquid petroleum gas used for cooking. These gases are heavier than air, so if there is a leak, they will build up in the bilge and can form an explosive mixture with air.

Being trapped in the accommodation is the most immediate danger from fire on a yacht, therefore the best place to stow fire extinguishers is at exits, so that you can fight the fire whilst keeping an escape route clear.

Petrol and cooking gases have a distinctive smell, but you can also fit special gas detectors that set off an alarm if there is a build up of gas. Make sure that there is a meticulous attitude to fire prevention on board. Switch gas and petrol off at the tank or bottle when not in use and pump out the bilges regularly. Also ensure that your gas appliances and bottles are properly installed and maintained.

Smokers are another fire risk so make sure that they carefully dispose of ash, matches and cigarette stubs and do not put the rest of the crew at risk through carelessness.

Fire Extinguishers

Page 12 has recommendations for the type and numbers of fire extinguishers for boats of less than 13.7m LOA.

There are many types of fire extinguisher available with different extinguishing agents to cope with various kinds of fire. Letters designate the type of fire that the extinguisher has been designed to deal with:

A - carbonaceous, eg wood, paper, bedding etc

B - flammable liquids, eg oil and fuel

C - flammable gases

The power rating of the fire extinguisher is usually expressed as a number, eg 5A/34B or 13A/113B. If in doubt, check with the manufacturer or the retailer. Most fire extinguishers can deal with at least two types of fire and some will deal with all three. Halon (which is a greenhouse gas) extinguishers are now not available and cannot be recharged. If you have a Halon extinguisher, you should replace it by 2003.

Dry powder is not recommended for accommodation areas. This is because the extinguishant can cause breathing difficulties and even impair vision if used in confined spaces. It also has a detrimental effect on electrical equipment, even though it may not have been involved in the fire. AFFF (aqueous foam forming film) extinguishers are recommended by the fire service.

The engine compartment requires either a fixed system or a system that can be directed into the engine space without opening the cover to the engine. The engine compartment should be boxed in with fire retardant sound proofing and should also be gas tight - A CO_2 extinguishing system is probably the best option, because although the initial cost may be high, they are cheap to refill. An alternative is FM200 but it is more expensive to recharge. The volume of the engine space will dictate the size of extinguisher you need, and so you should check with the supplier.

For general use, an A/B rating is required. You need to strike a balance between having an extinguisher that is small enough to use at sea, when conditions may be rough, but large enough to knock down the fire while water or a larger extinguisher is fetched. Extinguishers with not less than a power rating of 5A/34B should be placed at each exit from accommodation spaces to the open deck. There should be a minimum of two such extinguishers on board.

The Fire Service recommends that at least one 13A/113B 6 litre foam spray extinguisher be carried on all boats. This type of extinguisher is quite large and so stowage can be challenging on smaller boats. Alternatively, consider carrying smaller extinguishers adding up to the equivalent fire rating - suppliers will have details. This requirement is in addition to the smaller extinguishers that should be located at all accommodation exits.

Don't use water as an extinguishing agent on fires that involve liquids or electrics. It can be highly dangerous and even explosive if used on fires involving burning fat, petrol or diesel. Water is very useful for fires involving bedding or soft furnishings. These types of fires may appear to be extinguished but later break out again. Prevent this by soaking the burning material and its surroundings with large quantities of water.

Fire blankets

A fire blanket is very useful for dealing with small galley fires. They are quick and easy to handle. Site the fire blanket away from the galley, ideally on opposite side to the stove, so that it can be reached in the event of a fire.

In the accommodation areas ventilate to prevent fires and other incidents

Open flame appliances will produce carbon dioxide and even carbon monoxide. The dangers of carbon monoxide poisoning are well documented. Good ventilation is therefore very important, but strike a balance between adequate ventilation and producing so much that the gas flame blows out. This is particularly true of old style cookers and heaters that may not have balanced flues.

Charging batteries produces explosive fumes so ventilation is vital during this process. A submerged battery will produce poisonous chlorine gas.

Petrol and gas should be stored in a way that ensures leaks and spillages drain overboard and do not gather in cockpit lockers and bilges. If you can, store outboard engines and spare petrol cans on the aft pulpit. Gas and additional fuel stowage should always be stored in vented lockers.

PERSONAL SAFETY

Hypothermia and Cold Shock

It is nearly always colder at sea than ashore, and anyone who gets very cold risks hypothermia. This is a condition that reduces the ability to think and act logically. It can kill if not recognised and treated quickly. Being cold is particularly dangerous at sea because it is generally wet and windy too. Wind chill and wet clothing can dramatically reduce body temperature in a very short time. Learn how to recognise the symptoms of

hypothermia and know how to treat it. It is a good idea for all skippers do the RYA's First Aid at Sea course, (see pages 56/57) although any first aid course that deals with hypothermia is suitable.

Clothing

What you and your crew wear while cruising will very much depend on the climate and environment that you are in at the time. This book deals primarily with cruising in the UK and northern European waters.

Although cheap and convenient, lightweight shower proof jackets and trousers are just not up to the job. Heavier weight, specialist, sailing gear is definitely best. One piece waterproof suits are great for dinghy sailing but not practical for cruising as they are difficult to get on and off in confined spaces.

Every crew member should have boots, trousers, a jacket or smock and a hat or hood.

Head protection is both important for conserving heat on cold, damp days and for sun protection when the weather is fine.

Use a small towel (or similar) as a neck scarf. This will help prevent a good proportion of cold water getting down your neck and under your oilskins.

The best way to keep warm is to layer clothing - two or three thinner layers are more effective than one thick piece of clothing as they trap insulating air between them. If you are using breathable oilskins or waterproofs, wear complementary layers of clothing that breathe and wick away moisture. Clothing made of natural fibres will compromise the breathability and waterproof nature of high tech clothing layers. Manufacturers or retailers can give further advice.

If you are long distance cruising in winter, particularly in high latitudes, when the sea temperature is expected to be less than 10°C, each crew member should have an immersion suit.

Footwear should be non-slip. Many manufacturers offer breathable sea boots and deck shoes.

If you are working in the engine space, ensure that all loose clothing, long hair and harnesses are out of harm's way.

Lifejackets and buoyancy aids

There should be a lifejacket for every crew member on board that should be allocated and adjusted to fit before departure. Everyone should be able to identify their own lifejacket and know where it is stowed.

Make the rules clear about when lifejackets MUST be worn but also allow crew members to wear them whenever they feel the need.

Crutch straps are essential for keeping the lifejacket on when in the water and particularly during a man overboard rescue. Racing boats are required to have crutch straps on all lifejackets. Some lifejacket models may have them fitted as standard, or you may have to buy them separately and fit them yourself. When fastened they should be tight to a point just short of uncomfortable.

Spray masks and lights are also available on some lifejackets or as optional extras. Spray masks provide protection from drowning caused by spray, which is a real danger in even mildly rough conditions should you go overboard. Lights help to locate a casualty in the dark.

The RYA recommends that crutch straps, spray masks and lights are fitted to all lifejackets used on cruising boats.

There is quite a difference between the various classes of buoyancy aids and lifejackets. In general terms, a buoyancy aid is designed to keep a conscious person afloat, whereas an inflated lifejacket is designed to support an unconscious person afloat, with their nose and mouth clear of the water.

There are recognised standards for all types of personal buoyancy equipment:

50N Buoyancy Aid - EN 393

These are suitable for competent swimmers in sheltered water where help is close at hand. They are designed to support a conscious person who can help themselves. They tend to be made of foam and are designed to allow maximum movement for active watersports such as dinghy sailing, windsurfing, canoeing etc. They are not suitable for sail or motor cruising.

100N lifejacket - EN 395

These are suitable for swimmers and non-swimmers in inshore waters. They give some assurance of safety from drowning in relatively calm waters.

They are not guaranteed to self-right an unconscious wearer wearing waterproof clothing and should not be expected to protect the airway of an unconscious wearer in rough water. Therefore, they are only suitable for day sailing when close to land and in sheltered waters.

Like the 50N buoyancy aids, they tend to be made of foam. Children's 100N lifejackets should be fitted with crutch straps, to keep them on if the child has to be lifted out of the water, and D-rings to allow harness lines to be attached.

150N lifejacket - EN 396

These are suitable for both swimmers and non-swimmers. They can be used in all but the most severe conditions and they give reasonable assurance of safety from drowning to a person not fully capable of helping themselves. They may not immediately self-right an unconscious person wearing heavy waterproof clothing.

There are two types - air and foam, and air-only. Air and foam provide some measure of permanent buoyancy, but are much more bulky than the air-only types.

Air-only lifejackets are the most popular on cruising boats; particularly the compact, slim designs that do not interfere with normal movement. Many such designs also have harnesses incorporated.

There are various methods of triggering the inflation devices of air-only lifejackets; from dissolvable pellets to hydrostatic devices that are activated by water pressure should the wearer fall overboard.

275N lifejacket - EN 399

These are suitable for swimmers and non-swimmers. They are high performance lifejackets suitable for offshore and severe conditions where maximum protection is required. They give improved assurance of safety from drowning to people not able to help themselves. In the majority of cases they will self-right an unconscious user wearing heavy waterproofs.

This type of lifejacket should be used when high latitude cruising or when the crew are wearing survival suits.

Lifejacket maintenance

Whatever type of lifejacket you choose, it will need some basic maintenance. At least once a season, inflate all the lifejackets on board to check that they hold their pressure and to ensure that there are no leaks or damage. The trigger mechanisms on air only lifejackets may need basic servicing (eg. greasing the screw thread on gas canisters) and hydrostatic devices will need replacing at prescribed intervals. Reputable manufacturers will provide a servicing and repair service - speak to your retailer or the manufacturer for more details.

Safety harness

A safety harness gives protection from falling overboard. Lifejackets and harnesses can be worn together and there are also combined lifejackets and harnesses available. The standard for safety harnesses is EN 1095. Combined lifejackets and safety harnesses should comply with both sets of standards.

On sailing cruisers, as with lifejackets, every crew member should have their own harness, which is adjusted to fit before departure and they should know where it is stowed. When fitted, a harness should be slightly, uncomfortably tight to be effective.

On motor cruisers it is less important to have one harness per crew member, as it is unlikely that all of your crew will be on deck at the same time. The harness line hook can be one of a number of designs, but the safest are the locking hooks, which cannot be accidentally forced open.

As with lifejackets, crutch straps are essential to prevent the harness from being pulled off during a rescue. If they do not come as standard on your harness, seriously consider fitting them. As with lifejackets, all crew members should wear a harness whenever they feel that they need to (false bravado can be dangerous) and you should make the rules clear for when they MUST be worn.

Harness attachment points

Safety harnesses and lines are no good if there are inadequate attachment points on the boat. For instance, there should be attachment points to allow crew members to clip on outside of the companionway before they leave the safety of the accommodation below.

A jackstay running the length of the boat is also useful so that crew members can clip on before they leave the cockpit and remain attached until they return. Guardrails are not built to take the loads imposed by a safety harness and should never be used as attachment points.

When you are fitting jackstays place them as close as possible to the centre of the boat to help prevent crew members from falling over the side and not just to keep them attached to the boat.

On motor yachts, it is unlikely that your entire crew will be on the deck at the same time. However, there are special requirements for the attachment points on a motor cruiser capable of speeds over 8 knots. Anyone falling overboard from a motor cruiser at speed risks a broken back, so it is particularly important to have harness attachment points close to the centre of the deck to prevent this.

It is also important that the attachment points prevent the possibility of a casualty being dragged into the propeller.

LIFERAFTS

There are international standards for liferafts used on commercial ships, but at the moment there are none for leisure liferafts (although it is hoped that there will be in the future). Commercial ship liferafts have features in excess of your requirements as a leisure user and are extremely expensive.

The lack of a leisure standard means that there are a variety of liferafts available for the yachting market, which do not comply to commercial regulations and are not manufactured under the supervision of an independent authority. The International Sailing Federation (ISAF) overseas a minimum specification for yachtsmen's liferafts. Liferafts conforming to this are suitable for all area use. More details are available from RYA Cruising or RYA Technical (see page 47 for details).

There are a number of points to consider when you are choosing a liferaft:

Stability - a liferaft is a very small boat and has no fixed ballast. This means that its design has to prevent it from capsizing. Most liferafts are fitted with a number of water-ballast bags around the underside. These should be large, strongly constructed and fitted with a weight that will ensure they fill with water quickly when the liferaft is launched. The minimum is four water ballast bags, that make a total capacity of not less than 25 litres per person, or 160 litres, whichever is the greater.

A drogue, or sea anchor, is also essential for stability. Drogues are often made of porous material and have short shroud-lines to reduce the risk of tangling. The drogue attachment line must be long - at least 30m - and should be 6mm nylon. The drogue should be streamed as soon as possible after the liferaft has been launched.

Canopy - an automatically erecting canopy is highly desirable. As well as protecting the crew from cold, the canopy and support arch should prevent total inversion if the liferaft inflates upside down or is capsized by a wave.

Boarding aid - It is very difficult for anyone wearing wet clothes and an inflated lifejacket to board a liferaft from the water, particularly if there is no one else inside to help them. An inflatable step or ramp outside the main opening makes boarding from the water much easier.

Two-compartment buoyancy provision - commercial standards require this feature. Again, it is highly desirable, as it allows one or other of the buoyancy compartments to be damaged without compromising the buoyancy of the whole liferaft, and therefore the safety of the crew.

Inflatable floor - commercial liferafts must have a double floor, which is inflatable with a pump. This gives very good protection against the cold, although may not be necessary for relatively short period survival around the UK in summer. A partially inflatable floor, which provides an insulating ring around the edge of the liferaft where the survivors sit, is a good compromise.

There is a common misconception that a half inflated tender carried on deck can be a substitute for a liferaft. Although in some circumstances, (for instance, a fire onboard in calm weather) a tender could save the life of your crew it cannot be anything but a poor second best if the yacht has to be abandoned quickly or in any conditions but very calm weather. Rigid dinghies will capsize and float inverted in heavy seas.

Liferaft Equipment and Grab Bag

A full survival pack to commercial standards adds considerably to the cost of a liferaft. It is not strictly necessary for most coastal cruising boats since you are unlikely to be in the liferaft for more than 24 hours. A grab bag should be readily available to be taken into the liferaft.

The contents list below is taken from the DoT Code of Practice for Commercial Leisure Craft:

Suggested liferaft grab bag contents

Description of Equipment	Minimum Number
Second sea anchor and line	1
First aid kit	1
Daylight signalling mirror	1
Signalling whistle	1
Inflatable radar reflector	1
Red parachute flares	2
Red hand flares	3
Buoyant smoke signal	1
Thermal protective aid	1 per crew member
Illustrated copy of life-saving signals (see pages 50/51)	1
Pump	1
Paddles	1 pair
Repair kit	1
Recommended in addition:	
Sea sickness pills	Sufficient for the crew
Hand held VHF & spare batteries	1
Hand held GPS & spare batteries	1
In addition for some areas of the world:	
Food	Sufficient for the crew
Water	Sufficient for the crew
Warm clothing	Sufficient for the crew

Liferaft stowage

Liferafts are for emergency use and you must be able to deploy them immediately. This means you should either stow them on deck or in a locker opening directly onto the deck.

If you stow your liferaft on deck, secure it strongly to withstand heavy weather.

Hydrostatic Release Units (HRUs) can be used to secure the liferaft and to automatically release the liferaft when the boat is between 2 and 3 metres underwater.

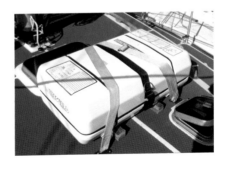

The painter must be secured to a strong point - it actuates the inflation device and so must remain attached to the yacht when the liferaft is launched.

Liferaft launching

It is highly recommended that skippers and crew members take the RYA Sea Survival course. It is a practical course that involves boarding a liferaft in a pool. It teaches liferaft drills and basic survival strategies. For more details - see page 56/57.

A liferaft is a last resort - it should never be considered as a better refuge than a yacht.

Never launch your liferaft until you need to abandon your boat. An inflated raft cannot be towed alongside for any length of time in a seaway without becoming damaged. Get all the crew into the liferaft as soon as possible to stabilise it and prevent capsize. Cut the painter once everyone is onboard and stream the drogue. Liferafts are virtually invisible to radar, so the inflatable radar reflector and hand-held VHF are invaluable aids to rescue.

Liferaft servicing

Ensure that your liferaft is serviced annually by an approved service agent. Servicing is expensive, but it is a false economy to compromise on it. Arrange to be present when your liferaft is being serviced so that you can actually examine the boarding arrangements and equipment it has.

MAN OVERBOARD (MOB) EQUIPMENT

Make sure that you have practised MOB procedures, that you are confident of what to do in an emergency and that you have briefed your crew on what to do too. There are details of MOB procedures in many RYA publications and RYA practical cruising courses teach MOB recovery techniques. For more information contact RYA Training - see page 47 for details.

If someone falls overboard from a boat travelling at 6 knots they will start to disappear behind wave crests within about 15 seconds. Successful recovery of a MOB depends on four basic elements:

- **Flotation** - The casualty remains afloat and is able to breathe

- **Location** - Finding the casualty

- **Securing** - The boat can be brought within securing reach of the casualty

- **Recovery** - The casualty can be lifted on board

Any equipment designed to be thrown to a MOB to help them stay afloat or to mark their position must be ready for immediate use. In the simplest form it should include:

Flotation
Lifebelts
A horseshoe lifebelt is designed to provide buoyancy for a person in the water. It therefore floats very high on the surface and drifts rapidly downwind. Fitting a drogue will reduce the speed of drift but it must still be thrown very close to the casualty if it is to be of any use to them.

Location
Automatic lights
An automatic light, either battery powered with a gravity switch, or with a sea-water cell, is essential to mark the position of a MOB at night. A light that is continuously on is more effective than a strobe light, even though it may be considerably less bright, because the line of sight from the yacht to the light will be obstructed by wave crests much of the time.

Dan buoy
A buoy fitted with a large dark flag on a pole that stands two metres clear of the water will help mark the area of the MOB. It should be attached to a horseshoe lifebelt by a floating line.

Securing
Heaving line
In a heavy sea, when there is greatest risk of losing someone overboard, it may be very difficult and hazardous to bring the boat alongside a casualty. A buoyant heaving line or a rescue quoit on a buoyant line is essential for making contact with a MOB. It is important that the line does not snarl or kink so it must be carefully stowed ready for use.

Recovery
It is not easy to lift a casualty out of the water and it poses a particular problem for a lightly crewed boat.

A boarding ladder will be a considerable help but only if the casualty is conscious and has not become exhausted.

A rope ladder is easy to secure, but difficult to climb as it will tend to move under the boat as soon as there is any weight on it. A moveable rigid ladder is easier to climb, but may be difficult to secure in a suitable position without special fittings.

A ladder permanently mounted on the stern, which can be hinged down to well below the waterline has the advantage that it is secure and is always ready for use. But, in a seaway it is not advisable to take the casualty on the stern at all because there is a danger of injury as the transom rises and falls in the waves.

To recover an exhausted or unconscious casualty some special lifting gear must be available or improvised. You, as skipper, should consider this problem and have a flexible plan for dealing with such an eventuality. Test the equipment (in a safe environment) to make sure that it is effective. Some ideas are explored below.

A handy-billy, rigged on the end of the halyard, and brought to a winch, makes it possible for a light crew member to recover a heavy casualty.

One of the greatest difficulties is attaching the handy-billy to the casualty. This is easier if the casualty is wearing a safety harness or lifejacket (lifejackets made to EN 396 and 399 - see page 29 - have a lifting becket for this purpose). If the casualty is wearing neither, you will probably have to send someone down a boarding ladder to pass and secure a rope around them.

A parbuckle can be improvised with a small sail and there are also a number of nets and slings available, which can be rigged as parbuckles. However, it is difficult to work out how to manoeuvre a casualty into the parbuckle when in a seaway.

There is specialist MOB equipment on the market that is designed to make securing and recovering a casualty easier and some of these have proved to be very efficient and successful.

Individual equipment to assist in a MOB situation

Your crew can equip themselves with various pieces of equipment in case they become a MOB casualty. As discussed on page 28, lifejacket lights are a good location aid for night or poor light conditions. Crew can keep a pack of mini-flares (page 24) in an oilskin pocket to help to identify their position.

406 MHz personal locator beacons (PLBs)

These can be thought of as miniature EPIRBS (Emergency Position Indicating Radio Beacons - see page 38 for more details), which give out a distress signal on 406 MHz to alert the Search and Rescue (SAR) authorities. Similar to 406 MHz EPIRBS, PLBs must be registered with the EPIRB Registry at Falmouth Coastguard (see page 47 for more details).

COMMUNICATIONS & INFORMATION SYSTEMS

Radio-telephone (R/T)

Most cruising yachts are fitted with a two-way radio and the majority of boats cruising UK and NW Europe waters will have a VHF radio-telephone (more commonly known as VHF).

Private pleasure boats are 'voluntary fit' radio users (ie, it is not compulsory for you to have a radio on board). However, because of the convenience and safety aspect of having reliable communication to the shore and other vessels, the RYA recommends that cruising boats do have a VHF radio on board. There are other benefits; the Coastguard transmits weather information and navigation warnings at regular intervals, and when you are within a port or harbour area you can monitor port operations frequencies or the local Vessel Traffic Service (VTS) frequencies. VHF also allows Search and Rescue (SAR) authorities to locate you using radio direction finding (RDF) equipment, should you get into trouble.

A cockpit loudspeaker will ensure that you can hear your radio above the noise of the wind and your engines.

Which type of radio?

VHF - this is a 'line of sight' communication and so has a relatively short range (maximum approximately 30 miles), but it is perfectly adequate for coastal cruising around the UK and mainland Europe. Fit the VHF antenna as high as possible on your boat, to maximise your radio's range.

When out of range of VHF, depending on where you will be cruising, either SSB/MF (single side band/medium frequency), HF radio (high frequency for high latitudes) or a satellite system will be suitable.

Satellite - there are a number of satellite systems available on the market, but INMARSAT is the most widely known. INMARSAT has the added bonus of being part of the Global Maritime Distress and Safety System (GMDSS - see below) and so it is linked to the international Search and Rescue system. There are a number of Inmarsat systems available. For more information, visit: www.inmarsat.com.

Satellite communications are pretty much global systems, although you should check your chosen system's coverage before you buy as they do vary. Beware - a number of satellite communications companies have suffered from lack of investment in the past, which has meant that they have suddenly gone out of business making their equipment obsolete.

Radio licensing

If you have VHF or any other R/T system on board for so called 'public correspondence', both the radio set and at least one person on board must be licensed.

Ship's radio licences and licences for hand-held VHF sets are available from the Radio Licensing Centre (see page 47).

If you have a VHF radio on board you should either have the VHF-restricted Operator's Licence (for non-GMDSS VHF radios only) or the SRC (Short Range Certificate). If you have MF, HF or Inmarsat equipment you will need the LRC (Long Range Certificate).

For more information about communications for cruising see the FAQs on the RYA's website, or the RYA book *VHF Radio (inc GMDSS), G22* (see page 58/59 for more details). For more information on the SRC or LRC operator's licences (VHF-restricted is no longer available) contact RYA Training, see page 47.

GMDSS

GMDSS stands for the Global Maritime Distress and Safety System. It is a worldwide system of communication and distress alerting via digital selective calling (DSC). DSC enables a distress call to be initiated before voice contact is established on the traditional radio distress frequency.

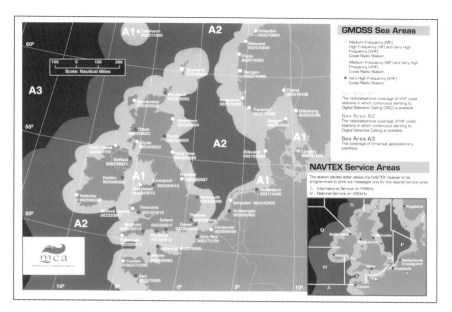

It also allows information, such as the position of the vessel in distress, and the nature of distress, to be passed as part of the initial digital message. This can dramatically speed up a Search and Rescue operation.

The UK Coastguard has declared an 'A1 area' operational around the UK coast - this basically means that VHF DSC is available in UK waters. For more information about GMDSS see the FAQs on the RYA's website or RYA book *VHF Radio (inc GMDSS), G22*.

Buying a radio?

All new fit radios must comply with both the operational requirements of GMDSS and the technical requirements of a EU Directive called the R&TTE Directive. You may be refused a licence for non-compliant radio equipment. There is more information in the RYA book *VHF Radio (inc GMDSS), G22*, or from either RYA Cruising or the MCA. As private, pleasure boats are voluntary fit radio users, existing radios do not need to be replaced.

NAVTEX

This is worldwide system that transmits weather and navigational information. It is part of GMDSS. Once you have programmed your receiver it will automatically receive and store (or print) information until you want to access it.

The 518kHz NAVTEX frequency is always transmitted in English, wherever you are in the world.

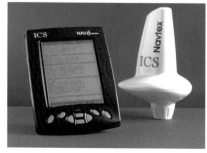

The 490 kHz Navtex frequency is reserved for transmissions in the local language.

In the UK, the Coastguard uses 490 kHz to transmit inshore waters forecasts and may expand this service to provide other information in the future.

Dual frequency sets are now available on the market.

EPIRBs

EPIRBs (Emergency Position Indicating Radio Beacons) are used to indicate distress and to help the Search and Rescue SAR authorities locate and home in on a casualty.

EPIRBs send a digital message to a satellite, which bounces it on to a SAR ground station. EPIRBs are a quick and effective method of distress alerting and particularly useful for long distance cruising when you may be out of radio contact with the shore, or if you are unable to send a Mayday using a radio.

Automatic EPIRBs are available. These are fitted with a Hydrostatic Release Unit (HRU). An HRU enables an EPIRB to float free and automatically activate itself, should your boat sink rapidly.

If you decide on an automatic EPIRB, the most important thing is where you are going to fit it. It must be positioned where it can be freely released should your boat founder, but protected from accidental damage by crew, or from being washed overboard or from being removed or stolen when the boat is unattended.

Because such a position may not be readily available, the most popular EPIRB for cruising boats is a manually activated beacon. This is usually either clipped on the bulkhead, just inside the companionway or is kept in the liferaft grab bag.

There are two types of EPIRBs available - 121.5MHz and 406MHz. The 121.5MHz is cheaper, but renowned for transmitting false alerts. By 2009, the frequency will no longer be used for distress, although it will remain a homing frequency.

The RYA recommends the use of 406MHz EPIRBs particularly for long-range cruising boats.

It is vital to register EPIRBs. Falmouth Coastguard holds the EPIRB registry (see page 47). Registration is easy and costs nothing.

SARTs

SARTs (Search and Rescue Radar Transponder) allow any radar-equipped vessel, including yachts, to pinpoint a distress call and home in on the casualty.

NAVIGATIONAL EQUIPMENT

There is now a bewildering range of electronic equipment available and it is tempting to rely absolutely on it. However, even if you choose to fit a sophisticated suite of electronic navigation equipment, your boat should still be equipped with a reliable compass and have sufficient up-to-date charts on board to cover your cruising area.

Never forget that any piece of equipment that relies on a power source can fail at any time.

Steering compass

Ensure that your compass is reliable and mounted so that it can be seen from any helming position.

Check compass deviation, which is caused by the magnetic influence of the yacht and her fittings, at the start of each season and whenever you fit any new equipment near to the compass that is electrical or contains ferrous metal. If you experience deviation of more than 3° have the compass corrected by a compass adjuster.

Compasses can malfunction - the liquid filled variety may develop a bubble in the liquid, and the bearing, on which the card is mounted, can wear or break.

Satellite navigation systems

Satellite navigation systems fix your position to a very accurate degree. The most widely and cheaply available system is GPS (Global Positioning System), which is funded and controlled by the US Government.

GPS may have revolutionised navigation for leisure users, but all electronic systems are vulnerable, particularly if they lose their source of power. Ensure that you can get yourself home using more traditional navigation methods should your GPS set fail.

The EC recently agreed funding for a European satellite navigation system, which will be called Galileo. It is not known if the EC plans to charge users for the service.

Charts

It is important to use up-to-date charts wherever you plan to cruise; navigation marks move, their characteristics change and physical changes occur around the coast.

The UK Hydrographic Office (UKHO), Stanfords and Imray all produce charts particularly designed for leisure craft use. If you use a GPS set, ensure that your charts are referenced to the WGS84 satellite datum, otherwise you will have to apply a correction to the position your GPS set gives.

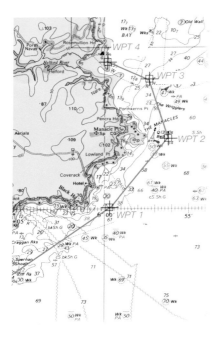

Alternatively, you can re-set the datum on your GPS set to that of your chart, before plotting your position on the chart. The UKHO or other chart producers can supply more information on datum shifts.

If you are using UK Hydrographic Office (Admiralty) charts, take advantage of their Notices to Mariners to correct your charts. They will then stay up to date for a number of years without costing you anything more. Notices to Mariners are available free on www.nmwebsearch.com with full details of how to use them. The RYA Cruising webpages include a FAQ on how to use Notices too.

Nautical almanacs, pilot books and sailing directions

There are a number of nautical almanacs available for the leisure market. These provide information on sailing directions, pilotage, tidal predictions, local sources of weather information and other important maritime information. This information is vital when coastal or offshore cruising and combined in one volume, it saves stowage space on board.

Sailing directions and pilot books are also essential when cruising off an unfamiliar coast. Commercial publications are available for popular cruising areas. A number of sailing clubs produce directions for areas not covered commercially. A full list is available from the Conference of Yacht Cruising Club's website (see page 47 for details).

FIRST AID KIT

When they first come on board, always ask your crew whether they have any medical problems that they take medication for (and check that they have enough medication with them) and whether they have any allergies or contra-indications that you and the rest of the crew should know about in case of an emergency.

The RYA runs a one-day First Aid at Sea course, which is ideal for all boat skippers and crew (see page 56/57 for details).

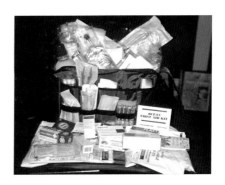

The list below is from the DoT Code of Practice for Leisure Craft. It is a list of minimum requirements, suitable for short cruises in areas where it is easy to replenish supplies. You may want to customise it. Store your first aid kit in a damp proof, strong, canvas bag or box and label it clearly.

Be aware that controlled drugs may not be dispensed without the permission of a qualified medical practitioner and that illegal possession could result in prosecution.

Suggested Minimum First Aid Kit

Item	Quantity required
Triangular bandages, with sides of approximately 90cm and a base of approx 127cm	4
Standard dressings, no 8 or 13 BPC	6
Standard dressings, no 9 or 14 BPC	2
Extra large sterile unmedicated dressings, 28cm x 17.7cm	2
Medium size safety pins, rustless	6
Assorted adhesive dressing strips medicated BPC	20
Sterile pads with attachments	2
Packages containing 15g sterile cotton wool	2
Large, disposable polythene gloves	5 pairs
Paracetamol, 50g tablets	50*
Seasickness tablets - hyosine hydrobromide 0.3mg recommended	50*
Butterfly closures - adhesive skin closures, length approximately 5cm, individually sealed sterile, in a container	20* & **
Forceps - epilation with oblique ends, 12.5cm, stainless steel throughout	1
Scissors - approximately 18cm, one blade sharp pointed and the other round ended. Conforming to BSI standard BS3646, published on 19/7/63	1
Thermometer - ordinary range clinical thermometer, stubby bulb pattern	1**
First Aid Manual - Published by St John Ambulance/St Andrews Ambulance Association/British Red Cross Society (latest edition)	1

* Twice these quantities to be carried in vessels carring 15 or more persons.

** Not required in area category 4.

Keep a couple of hot water bottles on board; they are useful for anyone who has become very cold on deck and can't warm up enough to sleep. Both extreme cold and fatigue can be very dangerous. Anyone suffering from a cold injury (such as exposure or hypothermia) should not be warmed up too quickly.

Medical Information and Supplies

The Department of Health publishes a booklet called *Health Advice for Travellers*, available free from Post Offices or their website (see page 47 for details). The booklet has information on everything you need, from immunisations for any part of the world, to malaria risks, and good tips for staying healthy when travelling.

If you are boating within the EC, complete Form E111, which is available free from post offices. Form E111 entitles you to free or reduced cost emergency medical treatment within the EC. The form must be stamped and signed by the Post Office, otherwise it is not valid.

The Department of Health advise investing in medical insurance for even the shortest trip abroad. There is more information about health insurance on their website. (See page 47).

GENERAL EQUIPMENT
Ropes and Fenders

You need a minimum of four mooring warps on a cruising boat. Two should be at least twice the length of the boat and two should be at least equal to the length of the boat.

You should also have a towing warp on board, although the kedge warp (see page 19) can be improvised instead. A towing warp should be at least 50m long.

It isn't possible to give much general advice on fenders. The very minimum for a medium-sized cruiser is four, but the shape of many hulls demands more. The larger a fender, the better it will protect your boat's hull, but in reality, size is limited by storage capacity.

Tenders

A tender is essential on all cruising boats. It's most obvious safety function is to lay out a kedge anchor. Tender size is a personal decision, but the ideal will carry the entire crew safely. Inflatable dinghies make it quite easy to carry decent sized tenders on cruising boats.

It is often said that more accidents occur in tenders than on the mother vessel. For that reason, all crew should wear lifejackets when using the tender - however short the journey. It's also important not to overload the tender, as it may become unstable and could capsize.

Drinking water

On a cruising boat, carry an emergency supply of drinking water that is separate from the main tank. Opaque plastic water containers are more algae resistant than translucent ones. In any case, emergency water should be renewed frequently to avoid contamination. Allow 10 litres per person.

Food and cooking

Hunger saps morale and strength and so, at the extreme, food can be a safety issue.

Cooking in rough weather is never easy and almost impossible in moving fast motor cruisers. Forward planning is essential. If the weather forecast is not good, then some pre-made food, and soup or hot drinks in flasks, will keep the crew going and no-one will have to endure too much time down below preparing meals in rough conditions. Prepare a hot meal before a long passage, so that it only needs to be heated up or kept warm to be eaten. Have lots of high energy, comforting snacks available such as sandwiches, chocolate and nuts, which can be eaten at any time.

SPARES

Companionways and Windows

Fit washboards for the companionway with a securing device that can be operated from either side of the hatch, so that they can be positively secured in heavy weather.

Carry a sheet of plywood, large enough to cover the largest window, together with bolts, strong-back and fittings. This can be cut down for smaller windows, as necessary.

Engine

Mechanical failure is still the most common cause of distress calls from both sail and motor pleasure vessels. The RYA's one day Diesel Engine Maintenance Course is extremely useful

and covers basic maintenance and simple fault-finding. See page 56/57 for more details.

Most engine manufacturers will supply a set of onboard spares, which you can build on and adapt as necessary. Always carry spare supplies of oil and grease.

On longer cruises ensure that you can get oil and other spares locally or carry enough with you.

Suggested engine spares include: engine and gearbox oil, drive belts, water pump impeller and gaskets, fuel filter elements, spark plugs.

Electrical

Carry a spare of every bulb you have on board, spare batteries for every item of equipment that needs them and spare fuses. If you know how to use them, carry a hydrometer, a supply of distilled water, a simple electrical circuit tester and various lengths of electrical wire.

Rigging

Suggested Rigging Spares

Item	Notes
Bosun's chair	
Spare hanks and sail slides	
Terylene thread, palm and needles	Needles: both sailmaker's and heavy domestic. Store needles in grease to prevent rust.
Replacement sheet	Of length and diameter to make a substitute for any sheet on the boat.
Spare halyard	Wire spliced with rope, if appropriate.
Length of wire	Long enough to replace any item of standing rigging, together with thimbles and bulldog grips to improvise end fittings.
Spare winch handle	
Spare batten	
Whipping twine and small cordage	For lashings.
Selection of spare shackles and split pins	

Tool kit

What you put in your tool kit really depends on your skills as a handyman.

Suggested Tool Kit

Item	Notes
Pliers	Both blunt ended and pointed.
Hacksaw	With at least 5 spare blades.
Screwdrivers	Large, medium and electrical sizes.
Set of spanners	All appropriate sizes, including socket spanners (or a socket set and ratchet) and an adjustable spanner.
Serrated-edge knife	For sawing through rope (or improvise with a bread knife).
Electrical connecters and crimping tool	
Glue	
Penetrating oil, WD40	
GRP repair kit	For a GRP boat. It should consist of chopped strand mat, resin, hardener and gel coat.
Sandpaper	
Puncture repair kit	For an inflatable tender.
Bolt croppers	Recommended for sailing boats for cutting the standing rigging in the event of dismasting, as an alternative to disconnecting the rigging at the chain plates.

GLOSSARY OF ABBREVIATIONS

BBC	British Broadcasting Corporation
BMF	British Marine Federation; the UK's marine trade association
CG66	Free safety registration scheme run by the Coastguard
COSPAS/SARSAT	A satellite system designed to provide distress alert and location data to assist Search and Rescue (SAR) operations
DSC	Digital Selective Calling (part of GMDSS)
DGPS	Digital GPS
DFT	Department for Transport
EPIRB	Emergency Position Indicating Radio Beacon; a distress alerting device that uses the COSPAS/SARSAT satellite system
EU	European Union
GLA	General Lighthouse Authority; comprises Trinity House Lighthouse Service, the Northern Lighthouse Board and the Commissioners of Irish Lights
GMDSS	Global Maritime Distress and Safety System
COG or C of G	Centre of gravity
GPS	Global Positioning System. A US Government funded world-wide satellite navigation system that is free to users.
HF	High Frequency
HMSO	HM Stationary Office
HRU	Hydrostatic Release Unit
IMO	International Maritime Organisation, the UN specialised agency for maritime affairs.
INMARSAT	A well known satellite communications company
ISAF	International Sailing Federation
LOA	Length overall
LRC	Long Range Radio Certificate
LWL	Length waterline
MCA	Maritime and Coastguard Agency; the Government agency responsible for maritime matters
MED	Marine Equipment Directive (Wheelmark)
MF	Medium frequency
MMSI	Mobile Maritime Service Identity

MSI	Marine Safety Information
MOB	Man Over Board
NAVTEX	Maritime Safety Information service, part of GMDSS
NTM or NM	Notices to Mariners
PLB	Personal Locator Beacon; a distress alerting device
RCS	Radar Cross Section
RDF	Radio Direction Finding
RYA	Royal Yachting Association; the UK's national association for all forms of sailing, windsurfing, powerboating and motorcruising
RNLI	Royal National Lifeboat Institution
R/T	Radio-telephone
RTC	RYA Training Centre
R&TTE	Radio Equipment and Telecommunications Terminal Equipment Directive
SAR	Search and Rescue
SART	Search and Rescue Radar Transponder
SOLAS	Safety of Life at Sea
SSB	Single Side Band
SRC	Short Range Radio Certificate
UKHO	United Kingdom Hydrographic Office
VHF	Very High Frequency
VTS	Vessel Traffic Systems

RYA	www.rya.org.uk	0845 345 0400
RYA Cruising	www.rya.org.uk/cruising	0845 345 0370
RYA Training	www.rya.org.uk/training	0845 345 0384
RYA Technical	www.rya.org.uk/technical	0845 345 0383
RYA Despatch (book orders)	www.rya.org.uk/shop	0845 345 0372
Maritime & Coastguard Agency (MCA)	www.mcga.gov.uk Email: infoline@mcga.gov.uk	023 8032 9100
Marine Accident Investigation Branch (MAIB)	www.maib.dft.gov.uk	023 8023 2527 (24 hours)
HMSO	www.hmso.gov.uk	0870 600 5522
RNLI SEA Check	www.rnli.org.uk/seacheck	0800 328 0600
British Waterways	www.boatsafetyscheme.com	01923 226422 or 0141 332 6939 in Scotland.
Conference of Yacht Cruising Clubs (CYCC)	www.cycc.org.uk	
Health Advice when Travelling (Department of Health)	www.doh.gov.uk/traveladvice	
Radio Licensing Centre PO Box 1495 Bristol BS99 3QS	Email: ams@ra.gsi.gov.uk www.radiolicencecentre.co.uk	0870 243 4433 (T) 0117 975 8911 (F)
The EPIRB Registry MRCC Falmouth Pendennis Point Castle Drive Falmouth Cornwall TR11 4WZ	Email: epirb@mcga.gov.uk www.mcga.gov.uk/flag/forms	01326 211569 (T) 01326 319264 (F)
Notice to Mariners:	www.nmwebsearch.com	

Small Ships Registry
Registry of Shipping and
Seamen
PO Box 165
Cardiff   Email: RSS_Renewal@mcga.gov.uk   029 2076 1911/8206
CF14 5FU   www.mcga.gov.uk/flag/forms/index.htm

Part 1 Registry
Register of Shipping and Seamen
PO Box 165
Cardiff   Email: RSS_Renewal@mcga.gov.uk   029 2076 8215/8219
CF14 5FU   www.mcga.gov.uk/flag/forms/index.htm

RYA SEA SENSE campaign

Cut your speed

Look before you tack

Watch your wash

Motor sailing is motoring

Look around & be aware

Be friendly - don't buzz!

Support your sport
get RYA trained

We're all in the same boat!

LIFE SAVING SIGNALS
To be used by Ships, Aircraft or Persons in Distress

Maritime and Coastguard Agency

Search and Rescue Unit Replies

You have been seen, assistance will be given as soon as possible.

OR

Orange smoke flare.

Three white star signals or three light and sound rockets fired at approximately 1 minute intervals.

Surface to Air Signals

Note: Use International Code of Signal by means of lights or flags or by laying out the symbol on the deck or ground with items which have a high contrast to the background.

Message	International Code of Signals		ICAO Visual Signals
I require assistance	V ✕	···▬	V
I require medical assistance	W ▣	▬ ▬	X
No or negative	N	▬·	N
Yes or affirmative	C	▬·▬·	Y
Proceeding in this direction			↑

Air to Surface Direction Signals

Sequence of 3 manoeuvres meaning proceed to this direction.

1

Circle vessel at least once.

2

Cross low, ahead a vessel rocking wings.

3

Overfly vessel and head in required direction.

Your assistance is no longer required.

Cross low, astern of vessel rocking wings.

Note: As a non preferred alternative to rocking wings, varying engine tone or volume may be used.

Shore to Ship Signals

Safe to land here.

OR

K

Vertical waving of both arms, white flag, light or flare.

Morse code signal by light or sound.

Landing here is dangerous. Additional signals mean safer landing in direction indicated.

OR

S: •••
Morse code signals by light or sound.
R: •—•
Land to the right of your current heading.
L: •—••
Land to the left of your current heading.

Horizontal waving of white flag, light or flare. Putting one flag, light or flare on ground and moving off with a second indicates direction of safer landing.

Air to Surface Replies

Message Understood.

OR

OR

OR

T OR R

Drop a message.

Rocking wings.

Flashing landing or navigation lights on and off twice.

Morse code signal by light.

Message Not Understood – Repeat.

OR

OR

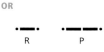
R   P   T

Straight and level flight.

Circling.

Morse code signal by light.

Surface to Air Replies

Message Understood – I will comply.

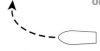
OR

T
Morse code signal by light.

OR

Change course to required direction.

Code & answering pendant "Close Up".

I am unable to comply.

OR

N

Note: Use the signal most appropriate to prevailling conditions,

Morse code signal by light.

International flag "N".

For information on distress flares and their use see pages 7, 11, 23, 24.

HOW TO JOIN THE SAFETY IDENTIFICATION SCHEME

IT'S FREE AND COULD SAVE YOUR LIFE.

- Complete the Safety Identification Scheme (CG66) questionnaire in ink and send it to the nearest Coastguard Co-ordination Centre.

- Enclose a recent photograph of your craft, if you have one.

- In return you will be sent an information pack containing details of other safety information and registration schemes and a card with brief details for your shore contact giving instructions on what action to take should they be concerned for the safety of the vessel/craft.

- This information will be entered on to a database and will be available to all Coastguard Co-ordination Centres. Its purpose will be to provide HM Coastguard with up to date details of the vessel/craft in a Search and Rescue situation and the provision of safety information.

- You will also be provided with a Change of Details Card.

- You should complete the card and return it to your Coastguard Co-ordination Centre if you change the name of your craft or any address given on the form changes.

- You should also return the card if the crafts appearance changes (colour etc), if there is any significant change to the equipment held or if you are no longer the owner.

- The Safety Identification Card is valid for two years. If it is not renewed within that time, it will be considered invalid and removed from the records.

ABOVE ALL DON'T FORGET THE COASTGUARD IS THERE TO HELP.

THE SERVICE IS FREE.

ISN'T YOUR SAFETY, YOUR FAMILY'S OR FRIENDS' WORTH THINKING ABOUT?

IN AN EMERGENCY DIAL 999 AND ASK FOR THE COASTGUARD

mca
Maritime and Coastguard Agency

SAFETY IDENTIFICATION SCHEME
(CG66)

DETAILS OF VESSEL
Name of Craft (Please Print):

If possible, enclose a photo of your boat

Where name displayed:

Sail or Fishing No:

Small Ships Registration No:

MMSI Number:

EPIRB Registration No:

Speed and endurance under power:
Knots   Hours

TYPE OF CRAFT   Sail Yacht ☐   Dinghy ☐   Motor Yacht ☐   Motor Cabin ☐   Sports Boat ☐   Inflatable ☐   Jet Ski ☐
Canoe/Kayak ☐   Sail Board ☐   Narrow Boat ☐   Barge ☐   Other ☐   (Please specify)

DESCRIPTION OF VESSEL
Type of Craft (Make/Model):   Length in metres: Draft in metres:

Colour of Hull above waterline: Colour of Hull below waterline: Colour of Sails:

Colour of Topsails: Sail Rig: Number of Hulls: Hull Id No:

LIFE SAVING EQUIPMENT
Liferaft (Make/Model):   Colour: Serial No:

Dinghy (Make/Model):   Type: Colour:

Flares carried: Number of Lifejackets: Colour of Lifejackets: Personal Locator Beacon:

Life rings carried :   Does it show the vessels name?:   Other:

RADIO/NAVIGATION EQUIPMENT
Radio: VHF ☐   MF ☐   HF ☐   Callsign: Channels: ....   **DSC:**   VHF ☐   MF ☐   HF ☐
Handheld: VHF ☐   VHF&DSC ☐   **EPIRB:** 121.5MHz ☐   406MHz ☐   GPS ☐   SATNAV ☐   Radar ☐   Echo Sounder ☐   SART ☐

DETAILS OF ACTIVITY   Usual Type of Activity: Usual Sea Area:
Where is boat normally kept: Berth ☐   Mooring ☐   Foreshore ☐   Home ☐   Stowage ☐   Address where kept:

DETAILS OF OWNER
Name:
Address:

Telephone:
Mobile:

DETAILS OF SHORE CONTACT
Name:
Address:

Telephone:
Mobile:

DETAILS OF CLUB
Name of Club or Association:

Telephone:

Signature of Owner:

Date:

This information will be used for Search and Rescue and safety information purposes only.
WHEN COMPLETED, PLEASE RETURN TO THE NEAREST COASTGUARD CO-ORDINATION STATION

MSF6000

COASTGUARD MARITIME CO-ORDINATION CENTRES

MRCC Aberdeen
Marine House
Blaikies Quay
Aberdeen
AB1 2PB
Tel: 01224 592334

MRSC Belfast
Bregenz House
Quay Street
Bangor BT20 5ED
Tel: 01247 463933

MRSC Brixham
Kings Quay
Brixham, Devon
TQ5 9TW
Tel: 01803 882704

MRCC Clyde
Navy Buildings
Eldon Street, Greenock
PA16 7QY
Tel: 01475 729988

MRCC Dover
Langdon Battery
Swingate, Dover
Kent CT15 5NA
Tel: 01304 210008

MRCC Falmouth
Pendennis Point
Castle Drive
Falmouth
Cornwall TR11 4WZ
Tel: 01326 317575

MRSC Holyhead
Prince of Wales Road
Holyhead
Anglesey
North Wales LL65 1ET
Tel: 01407 762051/
763911

MRSC Humber
Lime Kiln Road
Bridlington
East Yorkshire
YO15 2LX
Tel: 01262 672317

MRSC Liverpool
Hall Road West
Crosby
Liverpool L23 8SY
Tel: 0151 931 3341

MRSC Milford Haven
Gorsewood Drive
Hakin, Milford Haven
Pembrokeshire
SA73 3ER
Tel: 01646 690909

MRSC Pentland
Fifeness
Crail, Fife
KY10 3XN
Tel: 01333 450666

MRSC Portland
Custom House Quay
Weymouth, Dorset
DT4 8BE
Tel: 01305 760439

MRSC Shetland
The Knab
Knab Road
Lerwick, Shetland
ZE1 0AX
Tel: 01595 692976

MRSC Solent
Whyecroft House
44 Marine Parade West
Lee on Solent
Hants PO13 9WR
Tel: 02392 552100

MRSC Stornoway
Battery Point
Stornoway
Isle of Lewis HS1 2RT
Tel: 01851 702013/4

MRCC Swansea
Tutt Head
Mumbles, Swansea
SA3 4EX
Tel: 01792 366534

MRSC Thames
East Terrace
Walton-on-Naze
Essex CO14 8PY
Tel: 01255 675518

MRCC Yarmouth
Havenbridge House
4th Floor
Great Yarmouth
NR30 1HZ
Tel: 01493 851339

recommended
one-day

Diesel Engine Maintenance

Mechanical failure is the main cause of lifeboat callouts to yachts and motor cruisers. Basic maintenance and engine care will make sure that you are not part of this depressing statistic.

Learn how your engine works and how to keep it healthy by using basic checks and maintenance procedures. Examples of topics covered during the day are simple fault finding, bleeding the fuel system and changing the impeller. Most engine problems can be avoided by taking these simple precautions and most importantly you don't need any mechanical knowledge to attend this course.

Marine Radio Short Range Certificate

Using a VHF radio requires you by law to hold an operator's licence. This means that you know the procedures and avoid dogging the airwaves with unnecessary transmissions, which could block out a Mayday call. Digital Selective Calling (DSC) is an integral part of all new VHF sets. This feature allows calls to specific vessels and holders of the 'old' VHF licence will need to upgrade their qualifications if they purchase new equipment.

courses

For more information on RYA Training Centres and the courses they run, visit the RYA website: rya.org.uk/training or tel: 0845 345 0384 for a courses' brochure.

First Aid

In a medical emergency, a little first aid knowledge and immediate action can save lives, especially in remote locations. This course is designed to provide a working knowledge of first aid for people using small craft and to support skippers of yachts and motor vessels as well as RYA Instructors. The course is based on the recommendations of the Health and Safety Executive, and the Maritime and Coastguard Agency and includes all the usual first aid topics, relating them to on the water scenarios.

Sea Survival

Yachting is one of the safest leisure sporting activities and 99.9% of yachtsmen will never use their liferaft. However, if you are one of the unlucky few, your chances of survival will be greatly increased if you understand how to use the equipment and how to help yourself. The RYA one-day Sea Survival course is a genuine lifesaver. It covers how to use a yacht's safety equipment and includes a practical session on liferaft drills carried out in a swimming pool.

Radar

The International Regulations for Preventing Collisions at Sea state that if you have radar on board, you must know how to use it. The majority of motor cruisers and many sailing yachts now carry radar. Using practise simulators, the RYA one-day course gives you enough knowledge and skill to keep clear of navigational and shipping dangers.

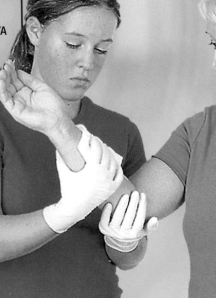

further recomm

ended
reading

to order any of these books,
telephone: 0845 345 0372
or visit the RYA webshop:
www.rya.org.uk/shop

expert
knowledge
and
advice
online

RYA
www.rya.org.uk

RYA *Membership*

Promoting and Protecting Boating
www.rya.org.uk

Promoting

The RYA is the national organisation which represents the interests of everyone who goes boating for pleasure.

The greater the membership, the louder our voice when it comes to protecting members' interests.

Apply for membership today, and support the RYA, to help the RYA support you.

and Protecting Boating

Benefits of Membership

- Access to expert advice on all aspects of boating from legal wrangles to training matters

- Special members' discounts on a range of products and services including boat insurance, books, videos and class certificates

- Free issue of certificates of competence, increasingly asked for by everyone from overseas governments to holiday companies, insurance underwriters to boat hirers

- Access to the wide range of RYA publications, including the quarterly magazine

- Third Party insurance for windsurfing members

- Free Internet access with RYA-Online

- Special discounts on AA membership

- Regular offers in RYA Magazine

- ...and much more

Join online at *www.rya.org.uk*
or use the form overleaf.

Visit the website for information, advice, member services and web shop.

If you have previously been a member and know your membership number please enter here

When completed, please send this form to: RYA RYA House Ensign Way Hamble Southampton SO31 4YA

	Tick box	Cash/Chq.	DD
Family†		£44	£41
Personal		£28	£25
Under 21		£11	£11

Please indicate your main area of interest

- ❏ Yacht Racing
- ❏ Yacht Cruising
- ❏ Dinghy Racing
- ❏ Dinghy Cruising
- ❏ Personal Watercraft
- ❏ Inland Waterways
- ❏ Powerboat Racing
- ❏ Windsurfing
- ❏ Motor Boating
- ❏ Sportsboats and RIBs

These prices are valid until 30.10.03   † Family Membership = 2 adults plus any U21s all living at the same address.

For details of Life Membership and paying over the phone by Credit/Debit card, please call 0845 345 0374/5 or join online at www.rya.org.uk

PLEASE USE BLOCK CAPITALS

	Title	Forename	Surname	Date of Birth	Male	Female
1.						
2.						
3.						
4.						

Address

Town   County   Postcode

Home Phone No.   Day Phone No.

Facsimile No.   Mobile No.

Email Address

Signature   Date

RYA

Instructions to your Bank or Building Society to pay by Direct Debit

DIRECT Debit

Please fill in the form and send to:
RYA RYA House Ensign Way Hamble Southampton SO31 4YA   Tel: 0845 345 0400

Name and full postal address of your Bank/Building Society	
To The Manager	Bank/Building Society
Address	
	Postcode

Name(s) of Account Holder(s)

Bank/Building Society account number

Branch Sort Code

Originator's Identification Number

9	5	5	2	1	3

Reference Number

Instruction to your Bank or Building Society
Please pay Royal Yachting Association Direct Debits from the account detailed in this instruction subject to the safeguards assured by The Direct Debit Guarantee. I understand that this instruction may remain with the Royal Yachting Association and, if so, details will be passed electronically to my Bank/Building Society.

Signature(s)

Date

Banks and Building Societies may not accept Direct Debit Instructions for some types of account

---

OR YOU CAN PAY BY CHEQUE

Source Code **023**	Cheque enclosed	£	Made payable to the Royal Yachting Association	**Office use only:** Membership number allocated